TALES FROM THE LIMESTONE

TALES FROM THE LIMESTONE

JOSH OSTER

Ellerslie Books

CONTENTS

AUTHOR'S NOTE

Tales from the Limestone is a culmination of many emotions. As I sit here writing this note, I wish that I could tell you exactly what I was thinking when I wrote the poems that you're about to read. What I can tell you, though, is that each poem stems from the experiences that I've had: from playing a gig on the weekend to witnessing the loss of our pet hedgehog, Tilly. Ultimately, I've tried my best to carefully give you an authentic view into the last decade of my life in West Virginia.

My Grandpap always said that everyone has to be themselves. That's what I've tried to do in this collection: be myself. So, as a warning: there are expletives. There is some humor as well as heartache (remember Tilly?). But, my hope is that you find some kind of interpretation in these poems to help guide you– whether you're celebrating your best moments, or you find yourself at your lowest. I think that's the beauty of music and poetry: to help us make sense of the world around us.

Pouring my soul into a book of poems–to narrow down my best memories, to revise each and every line–was a daunting task. But, I felt that it was an important one. West Virginia has always been my home. I've made (and lost) friends, found my amazing wife, and had some other mundane and exciting experiences. Regardless, it all happened right here in the Mountain State. Despite my best efforts to want to move to Ireland (it's beautiful, by the way), I'm grateful for everything that has happened to me here because they have not only helped me grow as a person, but they have also influenced the collection of poems that you're about to read.

Thank you for picking up this book and reading my story.

Josh

"Steeped in music, color, and images of the natural world, Oster's poetry provides windows into moments -- glimpses of emotions, of life and love, of fear and grief, of heartbreak and triumph. A stunning debut, in these poems you can hear a musician's voice singing a song that will resonate in some way with every reader."

--Jessica Salfia, author of *55 Strong: Inside the West Virginia Teachers' Strike*

"Josh Oster's poetry captures the intangible experience of being Appalachian. His work is hopeful, but colored by grief and despair. Those conflicting emotions are part of the Appalachian experience; Josh captures those feelings in this collection."

--Robert Dugan, author of *A Stranger Among Us: A Novel of the West Virginia Opioid Crisis*

Calico

the shadows of a Calico on the deck
A homeless wanderer, she nestles against the stone cold steps of the
    veranda
during a thunderstorm

Odd, it seems, how life is measured by the lead in your words,
the poison in your veins to scream at passing clouds.

Yet, the Calico will still rest her head in your lap.

Omagh

More and more
I feel at ease here
As notions of life across the
Atlantic
Bring back better times of happiness
Than the fickle
        Empty-handed promises
Of a tyrant at home.

More and more
She glances at me
Through some kind of liberty
That paralyzes the senses
Our kiss short, but never acrimonious
In Derry, our smiles protrude
Troubles pass and rebuild
On murals of love and trust.

More and more
This world around me
Never offers the superfluous anxiety of home
Yet keeps me awake at night
Wondering if ties can ever stay so true
When the tyrant at home
Threatens to ruin us all.

Downer

I lose sight of things
More often than I lose my
Keys
I lock myself out of so much

Mountaineer Eulogy

i'm from places of
needle point
relapses
places where my good friends struggle

i'm from places
where a twenty is the difference
from an empty tank
or a full stomach

i'm from every pothole in 495 south
to 270
to 81

until they're fixed
we'll go nowhere

Marigolds

Marigolds remind me of the deadheading season.
Mom, with shears of empathy, careful not to harm the roses,
gently snips
Brown and gold from her garden
Saving seeds
A fortune for another year

For years, she's kept her garden
A multitude of hearty foliage
A bedrock of limestone aches under what would be
Red mulch

A frog fountain
In the rock garden
Spits its disgust
At the dog days of Summer
And the algae on the footpath below

Ode to an Orange
Mechanical Pencil

Left behind on a desk
As cluttered as the headspace
You occupy
I write this message
To tell you that
Your lead breaks faster
Than my heart
On Sunday
Night,

the waning
Hours of the evening
Keep me muttering
Expletives
Because when i go to write my
Thoughts
Feelings
Emotions
Down to paper
My lead breaks

you've let me down

Spring

Rows of yellow seeds
Sprung across another field
Arduous labor
Catching the sunset
Better day's work
Left undone

On fishing

Casting hopes of good days In a lake of good fortune
The scent of pumpkin lures from tackle boxes
The scent of river,
A calm breeze sings low notes
And ripples it's body
Lichen on trees on yonder
Form symbiotic relationships

Ass in Coleman camping chair
Relaxation on the last few days of Summer
Yet, there's a fear
That a terror minder will soon call for
you
That responsibility will eventually nestle it's claws
work will call soon
dig its fangs into you

Forget it
Today's your day
To catch a memory
Hold it high A trophy
A title belt shot
Something that the White Marlin Open, Hell, even the passersby,
Would recognize.

Yet, all that's on the receiving line
Are branches, grass, and leaves

autumn

leaves change to auburn
saturnalia begins
collecting our bounties
locked arm in arm
to feast before frost
takes over
never mind the storytelling
we used to do over campfires, our skin,
and clothes stained by the smell
of soot and ash
that remained until morning
that acoustic guitar
that certainly played to wonder walled faces
that was better tuned for firewood
and a tinder song at best
there, we'd watch flames trickle until twilight
the upper echelons of stars
plotting their way, strategic
enough to shine, Orion
hunter and hunted
finally, sleep overcomes,
placing its hand on our
shoulders
it mollifies our empty labor
eyes close to frost

Island

False words flicker
Like candle light expectations
Burn out
Wax stuck to the fingertips
That stole dreams
And forced expectations

there was
too much
Red tape
to compromise

a found poem

From *Slaughterhouse Five* by Kurt Vonnegut

Everything was
Beautiful and nothing
Hurt
Kind of like the way they say you'll never amount to anything
Kind of like the way they say that you'll only be as valuable as
    the change
in the ashtray of your shitty '88
Hatchback

Funny when they had maserati dreams.

Titan

There's loneliness in the these hills that have swallowed me
Since age 5 knowing that
Comfort slips by
A Summer sun
A breeze from Grandpap's
Mountainside
Only gets to hang around for so long

I remember the vivid Peach trees from his place
Round, infectious beauty
The mist of pesticides
Urging the Aphids and the
Green June Beetles
That no vacancy Or hospitality
Would be found in these branches

The hiding place down below the mountain
A Shire to keep us safe
Between the stream amd the landing
Was where I learned
What gunfire really meant
Not a body cam realization
But the way my brother and I could bond

We'd trudge up the hill

From below our hiding place
After we'd finished filling soda bottles from IGA
With .22 rounds

I look back on these memories
After the mountains have eroded
To broken shale and broken hearts
A summer sun sets
And that breeze from the mountainside
Only hangs around for so long

To Grandma

Beautiful friends
seem to wish me the best
as my grandmother lies in a mahogany box
coupled with the static
of a chaplain's condolences.

Her emerald dress at this point
radiates the West Virginia music
of an American poet
who sang at her funeral.

I'll confess
that it was I that day
whose radiant guitar
shunned all fear and apprehension
as the multitudes and atoms of assumption
were sung in amazing grace.

failed haiku #1

Mondays suck life–
Dead end notions
Panic button
Five more minutes–
just to sleep

failed haiku #2

Bored and tired
Lavish frenzy-eyed
Skip ad to sell outs
On YouTube
To debts
From Hulu

Local Band Blues

Saturday night wrists
Bear those God. Awful.
Tight ass wristbands.
Worth ten dollars.
Worth it
When walls come down
And common ground's gained

Best friends are courage
That's drawn from the vein,
Sing. Scream. Defy.
What odds are left?

A mosh—waves
A current-electric
That screams
Though the speaker mains
Tell a different story

From the booze poured on
Slip on Vans
To the drunk guy
Who hits a vape
Who elbows me
Who hardly notices me

Just to ask the woman beside him
If she wants a hit
He side eyes me
Then pushes past me
To fanboy riches at the front of the stage

There's feedback in their monitors
A signal loop, fear on repeat
Until the sound guy
finally
Mutes their senses

Classroom

You chose to be here.
Knowing your voice
Is the difference
Between a
Future
And a pipeline prison
That they've been made to believe
Exists.

Help them defy it.

thoughts of a hedgehog

death is an inevitable truth
that makes algorithms quake
the news of passing and goings
are read, a listing for a new tenant

when you first came home
in a cardboard box of anxiety
i wonder
if you knew that this was comfort
a resting place to dig your claws into
to run rampant among your dreams

i wonder
when I held you
where you happy in the pocket of my hoodie?
a flash of peppered fury
looking to escape
somewhere, anywhere, hell under the sofa
would do
i'm just glad that I was part of your escape

i wonder
when I came in to check on you
at 10:30 PM
were you angry at me for waking you?

couldn't say that I could blame you
when sleep is a necessity
in an ever-changing world

i wonder
if you felt alone when you took your last breath
quills to the heavens, destined to strike
the fear of death from the sun
of a ceramic heat lamp
this became your final stand.

i wonder
if I would have tried harder
to be your friend
to be with you
would you still be here

your grave marks my failure
wrapped in Tupperware and a Walmart terry
fiber cloth towel
i was afraid to bury you
because I was afraid to leave you behind a part of myself can still feel
your cold as steel body
hardened, a forged sword buried

maybe, one day, I'll forgive myself until then,
Know that I'm sorry. until then, know that you'll still be
the hedgehog in that cardboard box
that I brought home years ago.

Snow Day

Heard the faucet tapping
In twenty degree weather
As snow fell faster
Barricading my soul inside
So nothing would freeze over

Find a way to make up
For lost time, a reflection
Of stir crazy emotions
In a frying pan of
What's left
Our rations are only as good
As a fit laden stomach ache

Only companion is four legs
We venture out for her sake
In blizzard drone attacks from God
Her snow laden fur
permanently marks this
Move by nature

Five Minutes

if I only had five minutes
I know for certain
That I'd find you in the end
Blonde meeting brown at the edge of your neck and
Your forehead
Glistening eyes that tell me a story
Or sing me a song
With fingers that carve their way around mine
Like some wisteria vine inching further and further
And lips that spill the enthusiasm
Of a never ending spark

Azul

You know that we've peaked
Or, by the grace of our manners,
plateaued
In the abundance of authoritarian abuse
When taking too much milk from
A cafeteria suddenly becomes a crime

To be eleven again
And imagine how the kneeling pressure
Of angst against my throat
Could fill my eyes with burgundy,
Hell, red filled eyes of ammunition,
Crying azul, llorrando por la atrocidad
Would make my skin crawl
Even today.

They blamed you
And took you away as an apostate
For simply living as a child

Navigate the Aesthetics

We sat down together underneath
that same painting
we loved it, grew envious of it
tormented by the scenic landscape
as beautiful as the Cliffs of Dover.
We navigated our minds around the aesthetics
wishing that it was hanging above the fireplace.

We sat there for hours, wishing that there was another like it.

Plot Arc

I am so tired.
This phrase seems to get stuck
On my tongue, quite often
Like a mantra
Or a tattoo idea
That my sleeve could bear
If only i wasn't so terrified of needles

I am so tired:
Of wishing the rust would free itself
Like the WD-40 we'd spray–
Dad and I
On squarebody trucks
That were going nowhere
A resurrection ritual
Turn key happiness

I am so tired:
Of feeling like having the higher ground
Only comes in a Star Wars movie
When a duel of the fates never aligns with my
Own Stars,
I'm destined to shoot them down
Scavenge them for the glow they have left
Just so I'll never have to see in the dark again.

I am so tired:
Because i have no ship
Only a sinking kayak
Like my first time on the shenandoah
Rivers don't scare me
But the thought of drowning does

The Outlaw

Do I dare shake the spurs of the tumbleweed at Sunset
Since he speaks of anger
with enough Hollow Points to penetrate the soul
and a smile to damn humanity?
Condemn him off the grid
you unfortunate pacifist
since he has the world on his side
he'll give you sanity
after the world has
turned
and
left.

Poverty in a Small Town

elegant graffiti litters October air
frost laden actions from a passer-by
create friction on the streets
another lonely vagabond with
a cart of aluminum wounds
views the world
in dotted lines
with no sense
of how to
connect
them.

a reminder about local shows

the intimate gigs
in makeshift beer tents
mean more than dollars
lost in silver pocket melodies

you had me at hell

sometimes I get the feeling
that it would be easier
to be less of a pessimist
when your light needs AAA batteries,
damn, i only have a nine volt.

Hitch Hiking

a poverty-stricken man
stuck out his thumb along the Appalachian highway
where beggars lice made its way
along silver guardrail and asphalt

he held the book of revelation in his hands,
read 16:12
down the waterway
driftwood on the other side of the guardrail
prepared for war

a passing semi up ahead
barks, its presence known
cb radio lingo
becomes a poetic form of its own

a poverty-stricken man
once stuck out his thumb along the Appalachian highway
who made his way past the boroughs of dogwood trees
wished he had never traveled alone

Smoke

The large white diesel pickup
blew a blanket of black smoke
out of its matter-of-fact chrome stacks
across the breathing air of the eastern panhandle.

Freya and Loki

humane society witnesses
will never tell you
how much a pur can calm
the senses
after losing them

life is fragile
delicate paws
of black and white
rest on your arms one minute
then tabby markings become
a road map back to
that place
where tales from the limestone
can break your heart
but can help you mend

that day
as we took you both into carriers of comfort
your wide eyes ready to see the world
marked
not only "gotcha days"
but days where I knew
i'd be better

where do things go from here?
hard to say
but as you follow me from bedroom to bedroom
jump from countertop
to stove
leaving those somehow muddy paw prints
that i always clean off
you've made room
for me to be vulnerable
for me to realize
that you've just cajoled me
into giving you another treat.

THANK YOU

Thank You

West Virginia has always been home to me. It's an even better place thanks to the individuals who helped make this collection and journey to publication possible.

Many thanks to H.S. Leigh Koonce and Ellerslie Books for taking on this collection and for giving me the chance to share my poems.

Jessica Salfia and the Spring Mills High School English Department: thank you for being so supportive and willing to check out some of these poems. Your excitement for this collection means a lot to me.

Rachel Hopkins, Amy Taylor, and Robert Dugan: thank you for helping me and supporting me throughout my first year of teaching. I will remember you all well.

Defending Cain: thank you for bringing good vibes to every live show that you put on. You were an inspiration for some of these poems.

Mike Snyder for contributing his amazing talents for the cover of this book.

Brandon Wright and the folks at Wright Live for all of the acoustic shows that you've allowed me to play on and to share my craft over the years. You're all great friends.

My band, Last Among Equals, for helping me hone my skills as a writer and singer. Here's to many more years with you guys.

Dr. Carrie Messenger and Dr. James Pate: thank you for encouraging my writing and poetry during my time at Shepherd University.

My parents, grandparents, and my extended family for their unwavering love and support for my art. You always encourage me to believe in myself.

To our cats, Loki and Freya: thank you for helping me process grief and loss. You will never realize how much you've helped me. So many poems are dedicated to you two.

To the O'Hagan family: thank you for welcoming me with open arms into your family and for always asking about me.

To my wife, Cheryl: you're my anchor. Thank you for always believing in my ideas, my dreams, and for going on that first date. You mean more to me than I think you will ever know.

ABOUT THE AUTHOR

A native of Martinsburg, West Virginia, Josh Oster is a poet, singer-songwriter, teacher, and husband. He teaches English and Creative Writing at Spring Mills High School. He also performs at various venues as a solo acoustic act as well as with his band, Last Among Equals. He currently lives in Martinsburg with his wife, Cheryl, and cats, Freya and Loki.

To keep up with Josh, you can find him on social media, @JoshOster-Music and @LastAmongEquals.